QUIET PLACES
of the
HEART

God's Reward from
Resting in Him

EUGENIA LOMBARD

WINEPRESS **WP** PUBLISHING

Packaged by WinePress Publishing, PO Box 428, Enumclaw, WA 98022. The views expressed or implied in this work do not necessarily reflect those of WinePress Publishing. The author(s) is ultimately responsible for the design, content and editorial accuracy of this work.

Unless otherwise noted, all scriptures are taken from the King James Version of the Bible.

Scripture references marked NIV are taken from the Holy Bible, New International Version, Copyright © 1973, 1978, 1984 by the International Bible Society. Used by permission of Zondervan Publishing House. The "NIV" and "New International Version" trademarks are registered in the United States Patent and Trademark Office by International Bible Society.

Scripture references marked NASB are taken from the New American Standard Bible, © 1960, 1963, 1968, 1971, 1972, 1973, 1975, 1977 by The Lockman Foundation. Used by permission.

ISBN 1-57921-478-9
Library of Congress Catalog Card Number: 2002106731

Thank You, Lord Jesus, for Rita Owen, Dr. Lois LeBar and Sharon Willmer, Your servants, who faithfully and lovingly taught and lived Christ's words to me, gradually and carefully, as I was able to receive truth and love from You through them. I'm so grateful for their time, prayer and giving of themselves to "make the wounded whole."

Contents

San Diego Zoo, Aviary and Bamboo

What spindly legs you stand on, little unnamed bird, with a white napkin-shaped muff about your neck and three pronged feet for better tread! Almost hidden among bamboo and reeds, you gain strength from a gray solid rock, where you perch to gaze at meandering tourists. Yellow flowers nod and wave in the breeze.

"Did you know, little bird, that bamboo can grow two hundred feet under the ground?" I whispered.

"Did you know, my lady, that I can fly all over this zoo without stopping once?" he seemed to reply to my vivid imagination.

"Why not let my imagination take flight a bit?" I mused. The little unknown bird and I would say in unison:

We both stand upon the Rock, Christ Jesus, and though unknown to this weary and restless world, we are well known to our Creator God, who watches over us and neither "slumbers nor sleeps" (Psalm 121:3-4). We are both made from the dust of the earth; yet perhaps in eternity we can be together because of Christ's blood and eternal life (1 John 5:11–12 NIV) as His gift to us (John 3:16). We both could wake at dawn to sing God's praises and sing again at the setting of the sun (Psalm 65:8b NIV). We can both be faithful in the little things, giving pleasure to our Creator and Sustainer. Though our vantage points be different—his of wider ken—yet we both take our pleasure in all of God's vast universe.

My brother called me. "Let's go to the lion house." I said goodbye to my feathered friend with beady eyes and a sharp bill. *I hope I can be as alert as you—quick to decide and swift in obedience.* Let me receive daily strength (Colossians 1:11, NASB) from the Rock of my salvation as I lean on Him while taking flight into unknown futures, where God already reigns supreme.

La Jolla Morning View

It was a reasonable time to go for a walk with one's 80-year-old dad. Nine-thirty was still a cool time as we meandered up Mount Soledad for a view of the Pacific Ocean, and we enjoyed seeing various trees and flowers en route.

"Dad, look at that tree! What is it?" He was ahead of me a few paces.

"Don't have the foggiest," he replied. Clipped, short phrases were his forté, with his New England upbringing and salt water in his veins from various sea excursions in his sloop, the "Triumvirate."

Dad kept walking ahead. I stopped in wonder.

"No leaves," I pondered, "yet gorgeous red blossoms of some sort." Silently, I wondered if there would be leaves sometime or if the tree was slightly blighted or had had its roots injured by some new construction. Lots of new homes were crowding onto good old Soledad.

"Lord, are my roots injured by some crowding or jostling down deep? Has the chaos at Christmas disturbed the Prince of Peace dwelling inside of me? Are my leaves still green, even in a year of drought?" Stillness is still needed for healthy growth.

Speak, Lord, in the stillness, while I wait on Thee;
Hush my heart to listen in expectancy.[1]

They will still yield fruit in old age; They shall be full of sap and very green, To declare that the Lord is upright; He is my rock, and there is no unrighteousness in Him. (Psalm 92:14-15 NASB)

O Lord Jesus, cause my life to be like a healthy tree (Psalm 1:3), with my roots deep into the soil of Your eternal love, growing in Your Word, feeding in the green pastures (Psalm 23:2), and being nourished by Your Holy Spirit. I long to bring forth fruit—fruit that will remain (John 15:16) so that Your name is lifted up among the heathen and Your glory is shown to a waiting world. In Christ our Lord, Amen.

---

1. May E. Grimes, "Speak, Lord, in the Stillness."

Wax-Wing Begonias

Mount Soledad, California

Not so long ago, before the drought, gardens along Mount Soledad's steep and winding roads were lush vibrant avenues of pink, red and white against the azure blue of the Pacific Rim. Watered at sunset, each blossom thrived on the night coolness. Succulent leaves retained precious moisture to sustain their plants during the blistering noon heat of the next day. The abundance of God's gracious provision was evident in the millions of tiny flowers, dotted with yellow centers.

"What is the lesson for me from this scene, Abba Father?" I whispered to my Creator God. *Pró* in Latin means "forth" and *fúndere* means "to pour," my dictionary informs me. So profusion would seem to be God's pouring forth immeasurably from his riches, his wisdom, his beauty, his colors and designs for us to enjoy bountifully. The word "succulent" has a root, "succus," which means juice or a liquid nourishment. I recalled the verse from John 15:1, "I am the true vine." My thoughts ranged out from this verse: I must remain in the vine in order to be nourished, to receive the flowing sap of God's creative juices, for resourcefulness, for wise choices and for Godliness. ". . . apart from me, you can do nothing," Jesus said (John 15:5b NIV).

O Lord Jesus, keep me hidden in You, receiving from Your Word, the Scriptures, moisture to sustain me for tomorrow's struggles, battles or drought. Give me Your abundant provision, protection, peace, perspective and perseverance. Without You, I am bereft. But with You "all things are possible" (Matthew 19:26). I look to You, my liege Lord. "God is our refuge and strength, a very present help in trouble." (Psalm 46:1) "And it will not be anxious in a year of drought nor cease to yield fruit" (Jeremiah 17:8b)—fruit which will *remain*. Amen.

Dusk, Near Herrick's Lake

Naperville, Illinois

The winter wind slowed to a whisper amid lengthened shadows across snow-covered fields and forest. The tracks of a lone cross-country skier disappeared into the horizon's pink-hewed shimmer. The crisp, cold Arctic air fogged my camera lens. Near and far blended together as the sun set, and I turned quickly toward the warmth of my car.

Sometimes our lives seem so weary that the near and far events blur with grief or sorrow beyond our control. With the death or near death of a relative or parent our emotions can dip and wane, like the setting sun.

O God, give me Your clear and perfect focus, Your viewpoint on troubles and trials of this passing world. Shield me and shelter me beneath Your everlasting arms until the night is over and the dawn of a new day comes.

I feed on God's faithfulness and His mercies, which are new every morning. I see the trees, snow, sunset and silence and "ponder anew what the Almighty can do, if with His love He befriend thee."[1] Another verse of this old hymn goes like this: "Praise to the Lord, who o'er all things so wondrously reigneth, shelters thee under His wings, yes, so gently sustaineth!"[2]

As I watch my aging parents gradually approach the valley of the shadow of death, I cling more and more to You, my Lord and my God. You hold in Your hands the keys of "death and of Hades," (Revelation 1:18 NASB) and You are "the resurrection and the life" (John 11:25 NASB).

O Lord Jesus, cause me to hear Your voice saying to me "Fear not, little flock; for it is your Father's good pleasure to give you the kingdom" (Luke 12:32). For You are my personal Savior and the Lord of my life, even of this trial. I cast this trouble upon You, releasing the weight of it, just as Your people were taught to roll their every care upon You, our great Jehovah. In Jesus' name, Amen.

---

1. Joachim, Neander "Praise to the Lord, the Almighty."
2. Ibid., stanza 2.

High Tide and Sunset

Bentwood, Cape Cod

"The earth is the Lord's, and the fulness thereof; the world, and they that dwell therein. For he hath founded it upon the seas, and established it upon the floods." (Psalm 24:1–2)

What a thrilling sight to watch the sun sink slowly and majestically into the sea—brilliant, golden, glistening upon the surface of the sea, and sending a tingle of joy like liquid love, flowing through my bloodstream. Every day God brings forth such grandeur for our eyes to feast upon. How seldom I stop the frantic pace and rest myself upon His eternal beauty. I must *choose* to fix my gaze upon Him—like David, who cried out: "One thing have I *desired* of the Lord, that will I *seek* after; that I may dwell in the house of the Lord all the days of my life, to *behold* the *beauty* of the *Lord*, and to enquire in his temple" (Psalm 27:4, italics added).

Help me, Lord, to choose what is lovely, to seek the beauty You provide, and to behold You in Your creation. Help me to focus upon the eternal—*seeing the invisible*—and reckon on You, the Living God, to keep my life on track with Your eternal purposes and the building of Your Kingdom. Then, from a place of restfulness, You can thrust me forth into Your harvest field, the world.

An old hymn from the Bohemian Brethren's "Kirchengesänge" says it best:

Sing praise to God who reigns above, the God of all creation.
The God of pow're, the God of love, The God of our salvation;
With healing balm my soul He fills, And every faithless murmur stills:
To God all praise and glory.[1]

O Lord Jesus, flood the surface of my life with Your pure radiance. Filter out the flaws. Enlighten my dreary labors and spread across the horizon of my life Your beauty of holiness. Strengthen me for tomorrow. In Christ's name. Amen.

---

1. Johann J. Schultz, "Sing Praise to God Who Reigns Above," tr. by Frances E. Cox.

God's Work

Ephesians 2:10, Cape Cod

Early to bed, early to rise, makes a man healthy, wealthy, and wise, the old saying goes.[1] It is true: we need both rest and work. Why? Because we are created in God's image and we are to be like Him. Does God work? "Come and see the works of God, Who is awesome in His deeds toward the sons of men" (Psalm 66:5 NASB). "Let Thy work appear to Thy servants, And Thy majesty to their children. And let the favor of the Lord our God be upon us; And do confirm for us the work of our hands; Yes, confirm the work of our hands" (Psalm 90:16–17 NASB).

God Himself works, and He wants us to work, doing what He has called us to do. "For we are his workmanship, created in Christ Jesus unto good works, which God hath before ordained that we should walk in them" (Ephesians 2:10). Because He calls us servants and friends; because He bought us with His own blood and forgives our sins; because He lives inside us, directing our paths, we can trust His power to work through us. "For the ways of a man are before the eyes of the Lord, And He watches all his paths" (Proverbs 5:21 NASB).

Let us pray: O Lord Jesus, work in me that which is pleasing to You. Keep me safe. Direct me with Your eyes upon me. Strengthen me this day by Your Holy Spirit. Amen.

Bear not a single care thyself,
One is too much for thee;
the work is Mine, and Mine alone;
Thy work—to rest in Me.[2]

---

1. John Clark, *Bartlett's Quotations*, p. 330 .
2. Dr. & Mrs. Howard Taylor, *Hudson Taylor's Spiritual Secret*, beginning of Chapter 1.

God's Way

Lan Tao, Hong Kong

Sometimes we lose our way in life's tangle yet long to unravel the twisted skein, knotted from troubles, trials, or turned out places. Yet "the Lord knoweth the way of the righteous . . ." (Psalm 1:6a) and His ways are higher than our ways (Isaiah 55:9) for "I am the Lord thy God which teacheth thee to profit, which leadeth thee by the way that thou shouldest go" (Isaiah 48:17). "They shall feed in the ways, and their pastures shall be in all high places" (Isaiah 49:9b). How God our Lord Jesus wants to protect and guide us.

"He instructs sinners in the way . . . He teaches the humble His way" (Psalm 25:8b, 9b NASB). As we see our sin we are humbled before Him. Job knew the process: "But he knoweth the way that I take: when he hath tried me, I shall come forth as gold" (Job 23:10). David's prayer was "Make me know Thy ways, O Lord; Teach me Thy paths" (Psalm 25:4 NASB).

What qualities do we need in order to have God's instruction? "Who is the man who fears the Lord? He will instruct him in the way he should choose" (Psalm 25:12 NASB). Wise Solomon wrote, "I guide you in the way of wisdom and lead you along straight paths" (Proverbs 4:11 NIV). So with the hymn writer we pray:

Lead me Lord, lead me in Thy righteousness: make Thy way plain before my face.
For it is Thou Lord, Thou Lord only, that makest me dwell in safety.
For it is Thou, Lord, Thou, Lord, only, that makest me dwell in safety.[1]

---

1. Samuel Wesley, "Praise the Lord, O My Soul."

Fruit Bearing

Blessed is the man that . . . bringeth forth his fruit in his season" (Psalm 1:1,3). Are you in process of fruit bearing—a normal, natural process like breathing? Is it your desire "that your fruit should remain" (John 15:16 NASB)?

In springtime, blossoms of the cherry, apple and pear trees are gorgeous in red, pink and yellow. The summer brings graded growth, sequentially. This is a purposeful process God wrought. In fall, the fruit is ripened by God's process, with rain and sun.

We also have been "Planted in the house of the LORD," and so we "will flourish in the courts of our God" (Psalm 92:13 NASB). We can "still yield fruit in old age . . . be full of sap and very green, To declare that the Lord is upright; He is my rock, and there is no unrighteousness in Him" (Psalm 92:14–15 NASB).

Keep me resting in You, Lord, today; still me with Your love. Quiet me with Your peace; flow through me by Your Holy Spirit. Equip me with Your resurrection life, and bring forth fruit for eternity. In Christ's name, Amen.

Let Him produce fruit through you and ask Him to teach you to abide in Him.

Abide in me, and I in you. As the branch cannot bear fruit of itself, except it abide in the vine; no more can ye, except ye abide in me. . . . Ye have not chosen me, but I have chosen you, and ordained you, that ye should go and bring forth fruit, and that your fruit should remain: that whatsoever ye shall ask of the Father in my name, he may give it to you. (John 15:4, 16)

A Beach Encounter

Clearwater Beach, Florida

The day dawned with exquisite beauty, as in a dream. My friends Lois and Mary and I drove to Clearwater Beach. As we drove along the coast, the ocean beckoned me to run and romp, to rest and repose. How fathomless the depths of God's resources, wisdom, and knowledge (Romans 11:33). The sky and sea seemed to scintillate with God's sparkling creativity! Delight swelled! "Oh, Lord God! Behold, thou hast made the heaven and the earth by thy great power and stretched out arm, and there is nothing too hard for thee" (Jeremiah 32:17). Gently, He began to pry loose concerns and cares from my heavy heart and contaminants of my thought life: the "how comes," "what ifs" and "whys" that needed to be dredged up, clearing the channel for the Holy Spirit to flow. *My child, I count the sand on the seashore, so I know how to unclutter your soul.*

I whispered, "Lord, transform my mind, will, and emotions. Unclutter, calm, and convince me of Your loving plans for me. I need You, Lord, to set boundaries for my thoughts."

We swam for hours that day, delighting in surf and sun. Thank You, Lord, for Your surgery amidst Your beauty—no lack, no want.

"For I will satisfy the weary ones and refresh everyone who languishes" (Jeremiah 31:25 NASB). The Lord delights in the way of the man [or woman] whose steps he has made firm (Psalm 37:23 NIV).

Take time today to find a place of beauty, rest and restoration for you. Let His Word fill the empty places and focus on His beauty. "God is my strength and power; and he maketh my way perfect" (2 Samuel 22:33). ". . . he considered him faithful who had made the promise" (Hebrews 11:11 NIV).

Lord Jesus, melt my heart today with Your infinite love; protect me by Your blood; guard my footsteps in Your paths. Feed me with Your truth. Amen.

Lan Tao Island

Hong Kong

The boat people of Hong Kong are a unique group. Their boats are their floating, compact homes, their offices, their places of recreation, their heritage, their means of transportation, their places of birth and—sometimes—death. Salt air, sails, sand and the smell of fish mingle in their memories. Lan Tao Island is an hour from Hong Kong by boat. As the tide ebbs and flows, wind-catching sails are unreefed for a day's jaunt toward the mainland coast. The haliards hang limp, with main and jib sheets cleated lightly; three masts are raked at a slight angle. Some family members are below deck; two are at the stern, and one at the tiller.

Their lives give cause for deep thought. They have no malls, beauty parlors, radar, computers, VCRs and e-mail. Instead, they have just brown sails, a wooden boat, a Chinese family without an address, P.C. or cellular phone.

The barren, marginal hills of Lan Tao remind me of how difficult life can be sometimes. "Lord, keep my life uncluttered and free to move at the slightest breath of Your Holy Spirit. Keep me poised to travel lightly, unfettered by clumsy contraptions which will perish with use. Let me hear Your directions clearly and obey them quickly, quietly and completely. "I will counsel you with My eye upon you" (Psalm 32:8b NASB). "And your ears will hear a word behind you, 'This is the way, walk in it' whenever you turn to the right or to the left" (Isaiah 30:21 NASB). "Is anything too difficult for the Lord?" (Genesis 18:14 NASB). Of course not.

Star Magnolia

Bloomingdale, Illinois

That cloud-covered early April day stood heavy, with cold winds and bleakness. The blue bells—harbinger of spring—and crocuses had sprung to life and were past their heyday. Now, the Star Magnolia had a slim chance of brightness. Each petal displayed a light, careful design by the Great Designer. Long before the leaves protruded from their sheaves, the pure white petals revealed their glory to a winter-weary world. Each spring the winds seemed to cut short their radiance; but this bush—hidden behind the garage—faired better than most.

Gazing out my living room window, I could watch the drama unfold. How patient God is! How tender! How varied His patterns, with such exquisite detail—beyond my imagination! How can I be that patient as I watch events, children and friends unfold in maturity before my eyes? How do I help each one find his potential and help and develop his character traits and talents? How can I encourage and yet at the same time challenge and discipline the younger ones? Will the winds of evil and sloth cut short their development? How can I protect the young ones from harsh and cruel malevolence?

Guide me O Thou great Jehovah, Pilgrim through this barren land;
I am weak, but Thou art mighty—Hold me with Thy powerful hand:
Bread of heaven, Bread of heaven,
Feed me 'til I want no more, Feed me 'til I want no more.
Open now the crystal fountain, Whence the healing stream doth flow;
Let the fire and cloudy pillar Lead me all thy journey through:
Strong Deliverer, strong Deliverer,
Be Thou still my strength and shield, Be Thou still my strength and shield.[1]

O Lord, though my life often feels as fragile as the petals of this Star Magnolia, hide me in the hollow of Your mighty hand. Protect, keep, strengthen, and guard me, for I am the "apple of your eye" (Psalm 17:8a NIV). ". . . in your light we see light" (Psalm 36:9b NIV). In Christ my Creator's all-powerful Name, Amen."

---

1. William Williams, "Guide Me, O Thou Great Jehovah."

Light

Church in Assisi, Italy

What is light? Is it a wave? Is it particles—a stream of particles flowing in a wave-like motion? How does it function? It clarifies, exposes, warms and gives life. (John 8:12)

"I am the light of the world," Jesus said. Light gives direction. "[H]e that followeth me shall not walk in darkness, but shall have the light of life" (John 8:12). "And the light shineth in darkness; and the darkness comprehended it not" (John 1:5). Those who are still in the realm of darkness cannot understand light. Light and life go together. So also do darkness and death. Light illumines and warms. We are commanded to "walk in the light, as he is in the light" (1 John 1:7 NASB). Light penetrates to reveal those things lurking in corners of our lives. The Word is "sharper than any twoedged sword, piercing even to the dividing asunder of soul and spirit, . . . and is a discerner of the thoughts and intents of the heart" (Hebrews 4:12). Proverbs warns us "[k]eep thy heart with all diligence, for out of it are the issues of life" (Proverbs 4:23). "[I]n your light we see light" (Psalm 36:9b NIV). We need the light of God to keep our ways pure, for it is the pure in heart that shall see God (Matthew 5:8). "The commandment of the Lord is pure, enlightening the eyes" (Psalm 19:8b). We desperately need His light to know which path to take in times of difficulty. "Thy Word is a lamp unto my feet and a light unto my path" (Psalm 119:105).

What does light produce? What results from light? Ephesians says, "For the fruit of the Light consists in all goodness and righteousness and truth" (Ephesians 5:9 NASB). I need to cling to the Lord Jesus at all times. David wrote, "The Lord is my light and my salvation. Whom shall I fear" (Psalm 27:1 NASB)? He also said, "They looked unto Him, and were lightened: and their faces were not ashamed" (Psalm 34:5). John, the beloved disciple, wrote of Jesus: "In Him was life, and the life was the light of men" (John 1:4 NASB). He is *still* the True Light that "lighteth every man that cometh into the world" (John 1:9). Bring each problem to Him and He will shed abroad His light upon it and give you His truth regarding it.

O Jesus, penetrate each area of my life with Your gleaming light to heal, nourish and purify me. Thank You, Lord.

Christmas Season

A Village Near Lake Atitlan, Guatemala, Central America

During one Christmas vacation, my mother, sister, and I traveled to a warmer climate for ten days. For two nights we stayed at a place on the edge of Lake Atitlan, Guatemala. A boat trip across the gorgeous lake brought us to this small village, where thatch roofs, stone and bamboo walls, earthen floors, palm trees and abundant flowers in profusion filled our view. This village had been without electricity, sanitation, medicine and schooling for generations—for centuries!

Can any of them read? I thought. *What is the mortality rate? Do they know the Living God and Jesus Christ, His one and only Son?*

We saw their places of sacrifice: earthen altars with dead chickens half burned on them—sacrificed to idols that could not hear or answer them. My heart sank, knowing this Indian village was way off the beaten track. "Whom shall I send, and who will go for us?" (Isaiah 6:8) "We all, like sheep, have gone astray, each of us has turned to his own way; and the Lord has laid on him the iniquity of us all" (Isaiah 53:6 NIV). "For Christ died for sins once for all, the righteous for the unrighteous, to bring you to God. He was put to death in the body but made alive by the Spirit" (1 Peter 3:18 NIV).

O Lord Jesus, please send Guatemalan believers to this village to tell them the good news of the gospel. Help them to understand Your truth and turn to You to have their sins forgiven and to have eternal life. In Christ's name, Amen.

Changes

A Tree in Winter, Wheaton, Illinois

God causes the changing of the seasons in nature, in our lives and in relationships. "[D]o not be conformed to this world, but be transformed by the renewing of your mind, that you may prove what the will of God is, that which is good and acceptable and perfect" (Romans 12:2 NASB). Seasons change; that's good! Though it is a "time to weep, and a time to laugh" (Ecclesiastes 3:4a) or "a time to be born, and a time to die" (Ecclesiastes 3:2a), I recall, "My times are in thy hand" (Psalm 31:15a) —the safest place to be.

Leaves tumble one by one. Fall is here once again. The tall aspens blowing in the breeze glint with sunlight's sparkling blaze. Homeward bound, I wind my way through these refreshing woods. Gratitude nourishes our souls with peaceful contentment, for "godliness with contentment is great gain" (1 Timothy 6:6).

Falmouth Harbor

Cape Cod

En route to visit an Oak's Bluff friend, I anticipated an adventure at sea on Martha's Vineyard Sound. Every day is precious, a twenty-four-hour gift to be unwrapped in sixty-minute segments. The blue sky heightened the crinkly blue harbor water. Sleek sloops and yawls resting at anchor whispered to one another of past adventures and discoveries around the bend of their futures. At 10:00 A.M., anticipation drew my heart and mind toward my waiting friends, Frank and Debby. A sail in the Sound awaited us, with Frank at the helm.

"Where does my heart find its home?"

"On the sea with the chambered nautilus," it echoed back.

"Forty years on the sea and then what?"

His voice whispered as the ferry headed out to sea, "I will never leave thee nor forsake thee" (Hebrews 13:5b).

O Lord, You are my true abiding place, my quiet harbor, my soul's anchor, and my protection from wind and waves.

> Stayed upon Your living breast
> I shall lean and safely rest
> Like a robin in its next,
> Only there my heart is blest.[1]

This old hymn came to mind:

> My faith has found a resting place, not in device nor creed;
> I trust the ever Living One, His wounds for me shall plead.
> I need no other argument, I need no other plea;
> It is enough that Jesus died, and that He died for me.[2]

O great Lord of the sea and sky, the heavens and the earth. Thank You for Your love, care, provision, friends, days of adventure and freedom and vacations. Most of all, thank You for Yourself. In Jesus' name, Amen.

---

1. Eugenia Lombard, "Staying."
2. Lidie H. Edmunds, "My Faith Has Found a Resting Place."

Knowing You will do the rest,
Do not put me to the test
Close to You—this is my quest
Whether home in East or West,
Jesus Christ, my only best.[3]

O Lord, the seas of life seem slippery to-day. Keep me looking to you as you take the helm of my life and carefully chart my course with your eternal compass and wise eyes.

"Trust in the Lord with all thine heart; and lean not unto thine own under-standing. In all thy ways acknowledge him, and he shall direct thy paths." (Proverbs 3:5-6)

---

3. Eugenia Lombard, "Staying."

Beach

North Side of Wing's Neck at Bentwood, Cape Cod

The rocky beach—with sand and seaweed interspersed—called me to come, play and rest awhile and to find refuge in the Rock that is higher than I. The lapping waves—gentle and inviting on the incoming tide—welcomed my bare feet and wriggling toes, just as they did many years ago when I was a toddler. On the bank, the white and pink roseragosa winked and nodded at me in the uneven offshore breeze. A blue, misty horizon softened the graceful bay as sailboats skimmed the surface, waiting for the afternoon race. Unused to walking on this pebbled beach, my bare feet complained ever so politely, and I sat to rest and scan the limpid scene of beauty before me.

His familiar voice called to me: "Come ye yourselves apart into a desert place, and rest awhile" (Mark 6:31). "I will never leave thee, nor forsake thee" (Hebrews 13:5b). How I love the gentle voice of the Holy Spirit—so comforting! He is called the Paraclete, the One called alongside to help. Yes, that's what I need—lots of help, Someone to come alongside of me and bear the burdens. "Like a shepherd He will tend His flock, In His arm He will gather the lambs, And carry them in His bosom; He will gently lead the nursing ewes" (Isaiah 40:11 NASB). "Save Thy people, and bless Thine inheritance; Be their shepherd also, and carry them forever" (Psalm 28:9 NASB). "Cast your burden upon the Lord, and He will sustain you; He will never allow the righteous to be shaken" (Psalm 55:22 NASB). "Blessed be the Lord, who daily bears our burden, The God who is our salvation" (Psalm 68:9 NASB).

My inner spirit cried out to Him whom my soul loves: Oh, Lord Jesus, keep me hidden under the shadow of Your wings; let me rest upon Your bosom; teach me to release to You the weight of this problem; help me to let You carry me on eagles' wings and bring me to the place of Your wholeness and holiness. Keep my inward being focused upon You, Your cross, Your resurrection and Your ascension. I love You, Lord Jesus. Amen.

A Protected Place

Painted Desert

Painted Desert—a place thousands of years old, with rugged rock formations, heat, snakes and dryness—near the Grand Canyon. I stood still in the shadow of a massive boulder, which towered ten feet above my head. It was boiling. His Word came silently to mind through a line from a hymn: "The shadow of a Mighty Rock within a weary land."[1] "For they drank from the spiritual rock that accompanied them" (1 Corinthians 10:4 NIV). "Nor is there any rock like our God" (1 Samuel 2:2 NASB). "The Lord is my rock" (Psalm 18:2 NIV). "Lead me to the rock that is higher than I" (Psalm 61:2 NASB).

I prayed quietly, "Lord, I need You to be a place of quiet, a reprieve from stress and a shade. This is a new endeavor for me; let me hide myself in You." I was extremely weary that June day. Four of us were driving from Chicago straight through to the Grand Canyon in a drive-away car. Our final destination was San Bernardino for six weeks of Campus Crusade new staff training. We constantly shifted drivers. The Painted Desert appeared barren, bleak and brutal in the noonday sun. After seeing it, we went back to our air-conditioned car, and on to California we drove.

Sometimes our lives feel barren, bruised, and bereft of fruit—not even a tuft of grass. "The grass withereth, the flower fadeth: but the word of our God shall stand for ever" (Isaiah 40:8).

O Lord, help me to keep looking to Your abundant resources and away from the dry places in my life. Help me to keep being persistent in appropriating Your promises. We drove on. Then I remembered a promise: "Therefore, my beloved brethren, be steadfast, immovable, always abounding in the work of the Lord, knowing that your toil is not in vain in the Lord" (1 Corinthians 15:58 NASB).

---

1. Elizabeth Clephare, "Beneath the Cross of Jesus."

Summer

A Stream in Spring, Breadloaf, Vermont

My brother was completing his M.A. at Breadloaf, Vermont. We drove up to see him and also visit friends in that region of hills, valleys and streams. We stopped by a roadside stream, cascading from the higher mountain ranges, bringing freezing, pure water in its flow. We quenched our thirsts and filled our thermoses.
A familiar hymn came to mind:

> Thou flowing water, pure and clear,
> Make music for thy Lord to hear,
> Alleluia!
>
> Thou rushing wind that art so strong,
> Ye clouds that sail in Heaven along,
> O Praise Him!
>
> Let all things their Creator bless,
> And worship Him in humbleness.
> O Praise Him![1]

My inner thirst—both physical and spiritual—was satisfied as I gazed upon the flashing sunlight reflected in the rushing rivers as they swiftly splashed their way downstream, glistening with summer light and sparkling with joy, making music for our ears and hearts. Let us allow the daily vistas to replenish and satisfy our souls as we traverse the valleys and hills of our given spheres of influence. Enjoy the crossings. Participate in the brief high altitudes of joy. Linger by refreshing streams and cool repose en route to our heavenly home—the city whose foundations are built by God, with streets of gold and faces of joy of people sorely missed. "We shall gather at the river."[2] "We have no continuing city, but we seek one to come" (Hebrews 13:14 NIV). We are aliens and pilgrims here (Hebrews 11:13). "I go and prepare a place for you . . . that where I am, there ye may be also" (John 14:3). "I am the way, the truth, and the life" (John 14:6a).

---

1. Francis of Assisi, "All Creatures of Our God and King," tr. by William H. Draper.
2. Negro spiritual, author unknown.

Play and Be Still

Fort Lauderdale Beach, Near a Friend's Condominium

Oh, to play in the surf, wiggling my toes in the sand and sinking into the receding swells! What limped luxury, with light bouncing off white foam and the Atlantic horizon seemingly stretched endlessly before my eyes!

Ah, summer! Ellen and Bob's condo has clean, white rattan furnishings and gleaming walls. As I relax there, my weary mind's feverish ramblings drain away. "Therefore, do not be anxious for tomorrow; for tomorrow will care for itself. Each day has enough trouble of its own" (Matthew 6:34 NASB), Jesus said. This was recorded by His disciple Matthew and through the Holy Spirit's choosing for our instruction so that we might become "thoroughly equipped for every good work" (2 Timothy 3:17 NIV) and activity.

Am I well fitted, proficient and complete for whatever He calls me to do today? Not with all these anxieties weighing me down. Help me, Lord, to release to You the weight of my anxieties and cease trying to carry them myself. Teach me now to let You sustain me and all the troubles together (Psalm 55:22). "Casting all your care upon him, for he careth for you" (1 Peter 5:7), the still small voice gently reminded me.

The tides of life ebb and flow out and in; often, it seems every twenty-four hours, and—like the ocean—sometimes even twice a day. You who sit upon the horizon (circle) of the earth (Isaiah 40:22). You, who observe all mankind, teach me to let go of my problems.

Your Son, the Lord Jesus, sits at Your right hand and daily makes intercession for us (Hebrews 7:25). Yes, He does this for me, Your blood-bought child (Colossians 3:1b). "Their strength is to sit still" (Isaiah 30:7b).

Oh, help me to sit still in Your lap as a weaned child. Leaning against You, may I receive strength from Your everlasting arms, which are always underneath me (Deuteronomy 33:27). In Jesus' name, Amen.

*R*eflection

A Log at Herrick's Lake, Naperville, Illinois

Herrick's Lake, Naperville, Illinois, is a restful, secluded hide-a-way with a simply sheltered open structure at one end and reflections of tree stumps on a still, early morning. The chilly crispness cleared my mind to meditate on God's wonders; God, the great Creator of wind, waves, raindrops and ripples, sight and sounds. He is the Potter and I am the clay. What will I allow Him to do with this clay vessel? Could I even become, someday, pottery for noble purposes? How can we become a clear and accurate reflection of His beauty, His truth, His light? "I am the way, the truth and the life," Jesus said (John 14:6).

The tree trunk's near-perfect reflection in the waters of Herrick's Lake caught my attention. Could I reflect my Lord's beauty and design with such accuracy and restfulness? *Help me, Father God, to portray You to others, so that they become thirsty for You. May they see You in me clearly, cleanly, purely, purposefully.*

"I raised you up for this very purpose, that I might display my power in you and that my name might be proclaimed in all the earth" (Romans 9:17 NIV). Thus we can become "pottery for noble purposes" (Romans 9:21) no matter our size or shape, age or heredity, environment or education. "But he knoweth the way that I take: and when he hath tried me I shall come forth as gold" (Job 23:10).

St. Peter's Square

Rome, Italy

The striking balance and symmetry of Bernini's curved Corinthian columns seemed to be reflected in the sparkling swish of fountain spray, caught by the winds of Rome. St. Peter's magnificent dome, the work of years, smiled beneficently down upon the crowds waiting none too patiently to enter the basilica. Works of art demonstrate to us years of planning, preparation and perseverance. All nations are welcomed here. Peter, around 64 A.D., wrote in a letter to the believers: "But you are a chosen race, a royal priesthood, a holy nation, a people for God's own possession, that you may proclaim the excellencies of Him who has called you out of darkness into His marvelous light" (1 Peter 2:9 NASB). Peter wrote to the diaspera, those scattered throughout Pontus, Galatia, Cappadocia, Asia and Bithynia (1 Peter 1:1), those who had accepted Christ as their personal Savior and Lord, who were at that time experiencing great persecution and suffering (1 Peter 2:4–5).

I considered all these historical events as I gazed upon the beauty of that square. *Lord,* I prayed silently, *give my life balance and symmetry in You, in Your Word, the Scriptures. Thank You that You alone are the fountain of life and in Your light we see light (Psalm 36:9). O Jesus, build up Your body, the Church (Colossians 1:18) and by Your word, teach, correct, reprove and train us in righteousness (2 Timothy 3:16). Build us as living stones into Your spiritual house (1 Peter 2:5), forgiven, cleansed, holy and pure, able to do what is right, by the power of Your Holy Spirit, working in us only that which is pleasing in Your sight (Hebrews 13:21). In the name of our Lord Jesus Christ, Amen.*

Atlantic Ocean

Cape Cod

It's one month before I move over one thousand miles from the old home to new ministry, new home, new opportunities, new steps of faith. Scanning the horizon, peering through the sea grass at the blue ocean, life seemed to be slightly out of sync, out of focus. The layers of my relationships were entwined with others in a variety of ways, some in the foreground and some in the background. How to determine the priorities for the day, this week and month, next year? Lord, only You know what lies ahead in my life. Help me move when You move, not before or after, but *with You.*

The people of Ezra's day said to him at a crisis point, "Rise up; this matter is in your hands. We will support you, so take courage and do it" (Ezra 10:4). O God, give me the necessary courage to make this move of one thousand miles. After thirty-three years here, to start again is hard for me, Lord. So God spoke to Joshua at a crisis point for him, "Be strong and of a good courage; be not afraid, neither be thou dismayed: for the LORD thy God is with thee whithersoever thou goest" (Joshua 1:9).

The old hymn floated into my mind: "Rise up, O men of God; Be done with lesser things; Give heart and soul and mind and strength to serve the King of Kings. Rise up, O men of God! The Church for you doth wait; Her strength unequal to her task; Rise up and make her great. Lift high the cross of Christ; Tread where His feet have trod; As brothers of the Son of man, Rise up, O men of God!"[1]

By the grace of God I am what I am. Isn't it wonderful that Jesus Christ is full of grace and truth? Lord help me to behold Your glory as I move forward in Your will one step at a time.

---

1. William P. Merrill, "Rise Up, O Men of God."

Dragon Boat Races

Hong Kong

A sparrow flew to the ground and started pecking here and there for food. Such a small creature, apparently insignificant in the greater scheme of life. We were watching the Dragon Boat Races from the shore in Hong Kong. These boats came from many parts of China to participate in the races.

God says, "It is he that sitteth upon the circle of the earth, and the inhabitants thereof are as grasshoppers . . . that bringeth the princes to nothing" (Isaiah 40:22a, 23a). What a perspective God must have of us humans! "Behold, the nations are like a drop from a bucket and are regarded as a speck of dust on the scales" (Isaiah 40:15a NASB). In heaven, He watches all: the sparrow, the boats, the nations and us. He knows and understands all at the same time, instantly. "He rules by His might forever; His eyes keep watch on the nations" (Psalm 66:7a NASB). Amazing! That includes you and me! He is in charge; He guides; He cares about the nations. "Ask of me, and I will make the nations your inheritance, the ends of the earth your possession" (Psalm 2:8 NIV).

O Lord of the Harvest, bring across my path today those hungry for You, that I might tell them about salvation through Your cross. Cause me to meet those of other nations whom You have prepared, those You are drawing out of darkness into Your marvelous light (1 Peter 2:9b). Make me sensitive to your instructions instantly so that your kingdom "shall reign wher'er the sun doth its successive journeys run."[1] O God, even now you can still "the turmoil of the nations" (Psalm 65:7b NIV).

---

1. Isaac Watts, "Jesus Shall Reign Where'er the Sun."

Papyrus in San Diego, California

Are you a weary weed in the swamp by the road, with spindly shaft to support your fan-shaped head? Or are you fit and shaped for king's use and pharaoh's pen?" The green papyrus have a long, illustrious history. The Funerary papyrus of Enus-Amun, in the Book of the Dead, was written in Egypt during the twenty-first dynasty, thousands of years ago. "Yet, you seem so weak, by this pathway, here in the San Diego Zoo. The One who created you knows all about you, your roots and stems and the time of ripeness and harvest. You may not sit by this forsaken path for long. You could adorn a palace wall. If you could hear, you might recall the famous words, 'The pen is mightier than the sword.'

"Did mighty King Solomon write parts of the book of Proverbs upon your great-great-grandfather's forebearers? Did Moses enscribe parts of the Torah upon your predecessors in antiquity?"

Sometimes weak and weary, I forget that God's plans are for welfare and not for calamity, to give a future and a hope (Jeremiah 29:11). Though I sit forlorn on byways, 'tis merely preparation time for proper use and seasoned ripeness. For harvest always follows seedtime. It is an eternal principle, physically, spiritually and mentally. Keep me faithful, O Lord, persevering with Your grace, encouraged by Your loving presence, being built up in Your Word, prepared for a palace wall, for influence, for obedience, for fruitfulness. For I am Your servant.

You are My friends, if you do what I command you. No longer do I call you slaves, for the slave does not know what his master is doing; but I have called you friends, for all things that I have heard from My Father I have made known to you. You did not choose Me, but I chose you, and appointed you, that you should go and bear fruit, and that your fruit should remain, that whatever you ask of the Father in My name, He may give to you. (John 15:14–16 NASB)

Prairie Path

Little Stream, Winfield, Illinois

The little stream in Winfield on that cold January afternoon breathed stillness, as clear reflection appeared to sooth my frayed nerves. I've heard deer come to drink here at dawn. Only once I heard the hunter's shots and shuddered half asleep in bed. The arching branches bend their outstretched limbs toward the water. Underneath that water-course, roots do the same stretching dance toward nourishment and satisfaction. Thirst assuaged, they stretch upward toward the sunlight. A pattern for rest and receiving lies open to me here.

How can I better reflect the pattern for rest which God desires for me? How can I increase my receptivity to His purposes for my life? "Be still and know that I am God" (Psalm 46:10). "Lift up mine eyes unto the hills, from whence cometh my help" (Psalm 121:1). "You did not choose Me, but I chose you" (John 15:16 NASB). "I will be exalted in the earth" (Psalm 46:10). "Come unto me, all ye that labour and are heavy laden and I will give you rest" (Matthew 11:28). The Spirit of the Lord brought many verses to my mind as I lingered there waiting upon Him for instruction and enabling.

Oh, Lord Jesus, keep me still enough so that Your glory can be seen reflecting through my weaknesses and infirmities. Help me draw up nourishment from Your wells, not broken cisterns, which hold no water, but from Your eternal Word. I thirst for You. I bend my will to Your will, perfect, good and acceptable (Romans 12:1). Transform me day by day into Your image, even as by the Spirit of the Lord. I say "Yes" to Your ways, purposes and plans, which are always higher and better than mine (Isaiah 55:9). In Christ's holy name. Amen.

Tired Old Winter Tree

Wheaton, Illinois

The brilliant sun shown in a near-cloudless sky, blue as an ocean at dawn, cold as icicles, making my breath catch and nostrils cleave together. The tired, old tree seemed to wince at the frozen tundra-like landscape. Twigs and limbs alike reached valiantly toward the sun. Hibernation time for animals, resting dormant season for saplings, and what for me? Everything seems still, asleep, frozen in time and space. A glitch? An error? Oh, no! Much more than that.

See those slender branches, slight bits of snow scattered here and there? 'Tis only spring asleep in her reposing garb. Pared to simplicity, skeleton revealed to naked eye. But search through to the sap, though cold, in a few months, will run fast and furiously through each stem and twig, bursting with energy to produce leaves, green and lush, providing shade for you and me. Another season, another time, another opportunity, which arrives faithfully every spring.

Is it a dormant season for you? Is prickling impatience posing precarious problems for your energy drain? Does "why this" or "not now" disturb your meditation? Let this too, rest awhile. Leave ponderous future to God's awakening call. Bend your sodden will to His wise will that knows the robin's call and the groundhog's shadow better than you do. He who calls each star by name and numbers the hairs on your head, can as easily know the seasons of your life and when to send His strength through your weary limbs (as He does the tree's limbs). Let winter have her season in you this day; His timing is always perfect. Keep me safe in this time of struggle, Lord Jesus. I am Yours. Amen.

Herrick's Lake

Naperville, Illinois

I walk in the woods in November. Leaves lasso my ankles as I amble along, finding fresh food for thought, amidst fall vistas, familiar yet fresh mauve, amber, burnt umber, grays of many hues come to view. The land rests. I am restless. *"Can you not wait for the season for your life?"* my Savior seems to whisper to me, His petulant child. Pamela Reeves' quote came to mind, "Faith is . . . refusal to worry when I haven't a clue as to what God would have me do with my life."[1] *O Lord, show me the little foxes which are spoiling the vine,* I cried in my heart. *"Be grateful,"* came the quick reply. "Lift up mine eyes unto the hills, from whence cometh my help" (Psalm 121:1). He seemed to be reminding me that spring cannot come before fall and winter in that order. These trees draw up nourishment all four seasons of the year. I too. His eternal springs are abundantly full, all the time. *"Drink, My child!"* Another quote of Ms. Reeves' came: "Faith is . . . Appreciating that my capacity to feel, communicate, think, achieve, choose, create, and commune with God comes from his making me like himself."[2]

Now my ninety-two-year-old mother is in a nursing home by her own choice. She's in the fall season of her life. I am frightened. Will she ever accept Christ as her Savior? So many are praying. *"Leave this, too, in My nail-pierced hands, child, and do not be anxious about anything. Trust Me. I love her more than you do,"* Jesus seemed to comfort me. I gave my mother into His hands, who died for her and longs for her to receive Him as Lord and Savior. Around another bend in the lake, I begin to hum a familiar hymn:

O could I speak the matchless worth, O could I sound the glories forth which in my Savior shines! I'd sing His perfect righteousness, And magnify the wondrous grace, which made salvation mine, Which made salvation mine.[3]

She accepted Christ as her Savior two weeks before she died January 2000.

---

1. Pamela Reeves, *Faith Is . . .* (Multnomah Press, Sisters, OR, 1970).
2. Ibid.
3. Samuel Medley, "O Could I Speak the Matchless Worth," adapted by Lowell Mason.

Lake Atitlan
Guatemala, Central America

Lake Atitlan, Guatemala, brilliantly reflected the sun's rays on that Christmas holiday vacation. My sister and I stood by the high dirt road, gazing at the vast panorama of gorgeous foliage, glistening water and majestic mountains. We drank in God's creative genius and love of color; the Designer's touch was everywhere! Later that afternoon we skimmed along the surface of the lake on the way to another village on the opposite shore. Our Lord Jesus walked along another dusty road by the Lake of Galilee, nearly two thousand years ago, telling His disciples how they could come to know His Father, their Creator, and how to have eternal life. These rough fishermen saw His crucifixion, His living person after the resurrection, and His ascension into heaven. They believed He was the only begotten Son of God, our Savior, and that He could set them free from whatever was binding them. They would turn their world upside down, going to many countries and nations to tell the good news of how men and women and children could be saved. I had been passing out many tracts in Spanish and longing for others to come to Jesus. In the areas we visited, there was much superstition, witchcraft and heathen practices. The poverty was frightful. Our eyes were opened to the tremendous needs.

O Lord, bring them out of darkness into Your wonderful light (1 Peter 2:9); You are not willing that any should perish; turn them from being dead in their trespasses and sins, to life in Christ (John 3:16). Open their eyes that they might see You, Lord Jesus, and come to know You personally, whom to know is life eternal. In Christ's name. Amen.

Lan Tao Island, Junk Boat by Mountain

Hong Kong

The ferry chugged along slowly on the calm China Sea that morning, passing junks of all sizes and shapes, doing various things. Mountain goats higher up the craggy slopes eek out an existence on marginal land. One junk caught my eye. Its sails patched, boom reefed slightly, a lady doing laundry on deck, preparing a noon meal of fish and rice, and at the stern, hung from the poop deck, several cages of wild fowl, gaggling their protest. During my one and a half years in Hong Kong, I'd seen thousands of such house-boats. *What happens in winter, Lord?* I mused. *How do they handle doctors, dentists, insurance, university goals, or prime time?* Of course, they don't. They stay in southern climes. Other junks are up north, in Swatao or along estuaries. Winter hinders precarious shipping routes, as the Apostle Paul experienced.

> Wild winds whirling
> Withersoever
> They wish
> Snow sunk swirling
> So much
> Sailing ships sink
> Tempestuous torrents twirling
> Turn on turn
> Tumbling trees twist[1]

The words of the Apostle Paul came to mind:

> The God who made the world and all things in it, since He is Lord of heaven and earth, does not dwell in temples made with hands; neither is He served by human hands, as though He needed anything, since He Himself gives to all life and breath and all things; and He made from one, every nation of mankind to live on all the face of the earth, having determined their appointed times, and the boundaries of their habitation, that they should seek God, if perhaps they might grope for Him and find Him, though He is not far from each one of us (Acts 17:24–27).

O God, will this family come to know You personally as Savior and Lord? Please cause someone to tell them Your good news so they can have their sins forgiven and receive eternal life, through You, Lord Jesus, I cried in my heart.

As the ferry landed at Kowloon, the millions of humanity overwhelmed me and yet God's heart was here to reach out with His truth, the Scriptures. *Make me a part of Your eternal purpose, Lord Jesus. I am Yours. Take me wherever You choose. Direct my feet in the paths You've chosen for me to take, 'til I see You face to face.*

---

1. Eugenia Lombard, "Wind's Choosing."

Lan Tao Island

Inner Lagoon with Barren Hills, Hong Kong

What a dreary, barren, forsaken place these islands seem in the early morning haze. We'd hiked for two hours, and I was hungry, thirsty and worn. The small inlet of brackish water fed a few small trees and carefully tended terraced gardens. Existence was minimal.

A "why bother" kind of place. Where would the trail lead next? Was there a trail? We checked the map. Yes, it was there. Only a footpath now. *How can people live in this place?* my thoughts jumped around inside my head. But God created this place and the people too, and He's watching them right now. He understands the hardships. There are barren, brackish and bruised places in my soul, too, which wear me out. I long for God's map and mastering of me. The "why bother" places in my life, He cares about, even when I don't or can't.

Cast on Him your every care
Jesus Christ is always there
Frustrations He will gently bear
Faithful He—do not despair!
Your ups and downs He is aware
Patiently His Name declare
You are His prize beyond compare
A jewel purchased and rare
He'll carry all your wear and tear
With His Spirit He'll repair
As you drink of His pure air
Of the world's ways do beware
Live for Him with flare
Your future is His affair
He's watching all birds in air
You are blood-bought and very fair.[1]

O Lord Jesus, carry me and my loads constantly, giving me more of You every minute so others sense Your strength and wholeness and be drawn out of darkness into Your marvelous light (1 Peter 2:9). Amen.

---

1. Eugenia Lombard, "Ups and Downs."

To order additional copies of

QUIET PLACES
of the
HEART

Have your credit card ready and call

Toll free: (877) 421-READ (7323)

or send $19.95* each plus $4.95 S&H** to

WinePress Publishing
PO Box 428
Enumclaw, WA 98022

or order online at: www.winepresspub.com

*WA residents, add 8.4% sales tax

**add $1.50 S&H for each additional book ordered